KRISTI

~~The Most Beautiful Girl in the World~~
By Timothy Downs

"I know romance isn't everything. I'm obsessing just the same."
- Sebadoh, Together or Alone

New Year's Eve

Soon, I hope,

he prays and hopes

through endless winter nights.

The blues sparkle,

frozen,

vivid in his heart.

He watches the traffic

puff and shiver past.

Rescue

We stood there
together,
watched the sun turn
from yellow to orange to red.
She said, "Well, I guess this is it."
I took her hand and smiled.
We stood at the edge of the world.
I'd been there before,
so I was fearless.
I'd been resurrected
two or three times already.
I was covered in scars and
they made me beautiful.
She thought herself flawless,
that 25 years of open doors and
complimentary drinks
made her unaccountable.
She thought she was innocent,
but she was wrong.
She was complicit.
She could have asked why but she didn't.
She could have looked down at the bodies.
She never looked out the window at night.
She chose to keep her eyes closed.
She was an accessory to these crimes.
This was my duty.
I was her goddamn hero.
I grabbed her wrist firmly and
pulled her screaming
into the sky.

Silver City

Driving through
the silver city,
I'm serenaded by Jeremy M. and
10 new songs.

Jeremy came up here, blossomed
from the grass and dirt,
this school, that lake,
these ancient streets.

(We all grew up here,
a long time ago,
on hot dish, comic books and
beer we stole from our dads.)

Today there are zombies outside HCMC.
Some of them just got out.
The rest are trying to get in.
They ache for blood and medicine.

On 37th Street,
2 African women shovel and struggle
to free their minivan
from the season's fierce, white paws.

I roll past taquerias, convenience stores,
Vietnamese restaurants, a pool hall,
another Target,
Bobby & Steve's.

Suddenly Jeremy is singing Paul W.'s song
about the skyway and
now look at this dumb bastard

crying in the rearview mirror.

I'm heading home.
I will burn incense.
I will offer tulips.
I will go on.

Sunday Night at Bogart's in Apple Valley

Michelle smiled and reached for

the microphone.

She was fearless up there.

She had lost count of how many

karaoke contests she had won.

She sang like Adele,

like Idina Menzel,

like Jennifer Hudson or

Katy Perry.

Her talent was undeniable.

Her sweet voice was a delicate monster.

She smiled and started to sing.

Everyone stopped talking.

They all turned to listen,

rapt, spellbound.

I felt kind of special,

as I was the only one in the room

who knew that

she was a

horrible

person.

Five Seconds

Everything can change
in five seconds.

I remember the first time I saw you.
I lived my whole life in a separate orbit until
this moment.

But now that our paths have crossed,
our lives intersected,
same room,
same time.
I see you,
you see me,
I am fundamentally different now,
chemically altered.

My eyes are HD and
they devour you.
My brain spins like a washing machine,
full of bubbles and chaos.
You smile at me and
my heart has an orgasm.

I start walking toward you,
stumbling happily
like a toddler trying to run.
Then he steps to your side,
puts his arm around your waist.
You turn and kiss him hello.

Everything can change
in five seconds.

Untitled

This thrilling panic.

My hand on the phone.

The possibility of you

Time Travel

I woke up this morning,
drank coffee,
fed the cats,
jumped in my car and

went back in time.
Nothing had changed.
Everything was different.
I went back to school,

walked the hallways
like a ghost,
like an invisible man.
I drove downtown and

stared up at the attic window
where we smoked cigarettes
and waited,
had sex,

made love,
made elaborate plans for
the future,
which turned somehow,

into this.
In the neighbor's backyard,
I had a somber, moonlit funeral
for Max, our parakeet, who

got sick and never got better
Love didn't save us.
I cried that night.
I said goodbye.

Heaven is a dream I had.
Time isn't real.
I got back in my car.
I drove off the face of your world.

Everything

Sunday evening,

100 degrees below zero,

I stare deeply into everything and

wait for a rush of bravado.

Yes, I was at First Ave last night

and I met a fabulous stranger.

She gave me this number and

I was hoping she was you.

High

The thrill lasts

an hour and a half.

You weave through your apartment

like a mouse in a maze.

If the phone rings,

you won't answer it.

No way.

Jesus, what if it's your mom?

What would you say?

The TV is an oracle,

one hundred voices of wisdom,

opinion and facts,

things you should really know,

from baseball scores to civil war,

from hurricanes to cartoon fistfights.

You cross the street to the store.

You feel brave.

You feel important.

You're way too high

to be out in public,

but the store is a safe place.

You carefully select Cool Ranch Doritos and

a fruit punch Gatorade.

The guy behind the counter asks,

How's it going?

You have to tell

someone,

so you say,

I'm so high.

He smiles and says,

Me too.

Smile Like Diamonds

When she was in the room,

anywhere in the bar,

he couldn't think straight.

his thoughts swerved out of control.

His eyes ached to see her,

to look across the room and see

that face, those eyes,

a smile like diamonds.

He wanted to explain that he was

so much more than a waiter

serving lunch, dinner and drinks

to indifferent strangers.

He was a poet, for God's sake,

a singer, a writer, an artist.

He saw her and the sweet hurricane

screaming in his heart was everything.

He wanted to know her details,

anything about her.

What colors did she wear,

what musicians and magazines?

What movies, what books, and

might she dig a small dose of poetry?

She kept beautiful secrets

in a separate world.

Growing Up

That winter I

crawled into the corner and

assumed the fetal position

until spring,

breaking only for

long weekends of

adolescent mayhem.

I woke up bruised.

There was blood on the pillow,

due to my terminal inability

to navigate

hallways, steps,

furniture and

you.

Motion and Peace

I.
Of course I'm self-absorbed.
I'm the only one here
(the only one leaving).
Driving through sunlight,
yesterday seems like years ago.
I race toward the river.
I'm a no-good stoner outlaw
on a moody, mindless mission.
I need to see my grandma's house.
I walk past antique shops,
churches and cafes,
the radio my shadow.
A blast of hot, red wind
reminds me of the dreams I had,
ice cream and picnics,
kickball, cousins and campers.
Children smile and scream as
Sunday school balloons
escape to heaven.

II.
I've been here forever
like those steeples in the sky.
I was a prince
before the land became a country.
I'm part of everything and I
chose the distance between us.
I found my family at the graveyard.
I discovered eternity there,
then drove away
into teenage autumn.

Rev Lover

"Yeah, I used to smoke that shit,"
Rev Lover says to me, almost casually,
in the corner of a smoky bar.
"In the morning, with the sun on my face,
I'd greet God and all his magic
with a big, fat one,
some coffee and
a cigarette.
Then I'd walk down to Walgreen's for a paper
and maybe
some orange juice and the dawn?
The dawn was a cool, summer breeze."
I nod.
I hold my breath, waiting.
"I don't need to take anything
to feel that way anymore, though."
He turns and looks at me for the first time
and says, "I guess I just don't feel that way
anymore."
He's drinking a bottle of water and
the music follows him everywhere, but
some time ago he gave up dancing as well.
Rev leans back against a pinball machine and
watches with faraway eyes.
"Nope, I don't do that shit anymore," he says
to no one and everyone and I'm the only one
who notices as he escapes into the night.

Gilligan

Look.

All I'm sayin' is,

if I had been on that island,

for that long,

with those two women,

I'm pretty sure

there would have been

babies

everywhere.

Inside

Hell yes, I'm as real as you.

I have pain too.

I live in a Cure song:

candles, cheap wine,

a black and white TV.

I get off on that.

I'm into angst, desire and oblivion,

digging this empty warehouse,

a lost corner of the city,

blue smoke and naked emotion.

I want more now,

stoned serious, sad and strong.

Pictures of me,

I bought this pain.

I'm drowning now.

I keep ice cubes in my poison.

There are cheese sandwiches for dinner.

I smoke a stole cigarette.

The sun shines in my dreams of dying.

Tell me, where is the glamour

in old tapes, dirty clothes,

a silent phone.

It's always Halloween on 17th St.

How can I kill this devil inside?

Jessica's Machine

"I'm just not sure he's right for you,"

I say to Jessica's machine at 3 AM on Sunday.

Would this guy write delicious,

delirious poetry in your honor?

Would he compose songs like silk

shadows on a gleaming guitar?

Would he give you sugar kisses

until flowers exploded inside you?

Jessica's machine remembers everything,

beeps "good night," leaves me dreaming.

She

Do you like my body?
she whispered
as I lay there,
shivering with joy.

I need it now,
I answered,
like air or water or food.
I cannot live without it.

Our life together was
rosy, warm, delicious,
like a love song raining
from the sky.

Small Things

Take the small things.

Little sips of poison

can kill a man.

Tiny little bullets

can make your head explode.

Three little words

can rescue you:

"I'm leaving now."

"I love you."

"Let's get high."

A song on the radio.

The way you make breakfast

in your underwear.

A pocket bible.

A photograph of 1968

gathering dust

on a bookshelf.

Small things

comprise the universe.

Small things.

A kitten.

A diamond.

Small things.

A pencil.

A golf ball.

A remote control

that turns off the sun.

Heaven

Can you tell that you're in heaven

on a golden hill like this?

I am so awake. I'm

on a postcard. Do you

still lose yourself?

I can see the ocean from here.

Sweet, soft, sexy guitars surround

me and I

might go even higher today.

I'm not afraid anymore because

my heart always bounces back and

I taught my soul indifference.

We are nonchalant.

We are serene,

This is where the joy is:

In the cool sun of October and

the clean, white pages I carry.

Perfect

You would be

perfect if

you were

here.

Middle School

Minnehaha Middle School,
grades 5 through 8.

We had ugly brown and yellow tote bags
for our gym clothes.

We were the first class to use
the new band room,

the new locker room,
classrooms and library.

I had Mrs. Sega,
then Mr. Schreyer,

then B.J. and finally Black Joe.
These were my homeroom teachers.

I was in love with both the Widen girls
cos they were twins

(Cindi and Wendy) and
I couldn't tell them apart.

I had my dad for band.
I wanted to play the drums, but

he said, I've got ten drummers already.
You'll play the French horn.

Thank God for basketball
at Minnehaha Middle School.

Hank Skid

No really,
Do the math.

The agency said my
father was 6 feet tall,

not married to my mother,
volatile,

charismatic but
not social.

They had drinks
on a Sunday night

a week before
Valentine's Day,

told each other stories,
daydream confessions and

dirty sweet talk.
Then dad blew a poem up inside her.

Here I am.

Misfit Toys

Live your life, love your wife,

carve your heart out with a knife.

Look the devil in the eye,

Say, "We are not afraid to die."

Say your prayers all day long.

Put your prayers into a song.

Sing your song out in the street.

Find a drummer, add a beat.

Remember what your parents taught you.

Do the things that they said not to.

You crash and burn. You live and learn.

This is life and it's your turn.

If you're not growing, then you're dying.

We're so happy that we're crying

tears of joy. Girls and boys,

we are all just misfit toys.

Remember that our lives are now.

today, this moment. Try somehow

to live your life, love your wife,

carve your heart out with a knife.

What Ashley Said

Every Sunday morning,

22-year-old babies

text each other relentlessly

about the things that happened last night,

like it matters somehow.

But I don't care

what Ashley said.

I don't care

if you got sick or

got laid or

lost your car keys at the bar.

None of it matters

unless

you got shot

or

fell in love.

Roses and Moonlight

"She's beautiful,"

whispered one rose

to the others.

I smiled.

You lay sleeping.

Big Baby

At this very moment,
in a chilly duplex some-
where near Como Ave SE,
a very old boy
stands in the kitchen,
in dirty socks and
a pair of black basketball shorts,
pouring half beers from red Solo cups
into a Miller Lite pitcher.

He doesn't feel sick
yet,
but he's getting there.
The secret is to re-fuel
before the symptoms present.
He fashions a full pitcher
from last night's flat beer and spit,
puts it in the fridge to chill,
digs out two cold bottles of Old Milwaukee
stashed under a bag of apples
in the crisper drawer,
turns on the TV in the living room
quietly.

(There are people still sleeping.
This is not his home,
but he tries to live here.)

He takes a fat chug of medicine,
a big baby with a bottle
who started to die
the day he was born.

8 AM October

8 AM October.
a gorgeous Italian girl on the Crosstown,

she in the black Jetta,
me in the silver Honda

We made eye contact,
smiled, said "Hi."

I asked, "How are you?"
"Good," she replied.

Then I looked back to
the road in front of me.

She faded left.
went south and

gone forever.
This was a single moment

a thousand years ago.
I keep it close to me.

I play it again and I wait
for 8 AM October.

Funeral

It was way over 90 degrees.

I had a black jacket in the backseat.

I was late and then

a wrong turn left me

steaming in a drenched sunset

at the end of the street.

Inside the church,

I stood carefully on the edge and

watched an angel offer

lemonade and brownies.

We listened to the stories and

then stood and cheered for Brian,

the laughter and the loss.

I drove 90 miles an hour to get there.

my eyes glazed and red like always,

while sour, summer clouds swirled and waited.

I bent an elbow out the window,

turned the radio on,

aimed my miniature sports car

toward the deep end.

November Skies

I have a picture on my dresser of

an innocent tourist.

My dream girl has a plain, old boyfriend who

hasn't fucked up

yet,

and she knows she's my dream girl.

I tried to talk to this bartender named Nikki but

I couldn't think straight.

I bought a guitar for my salvation.

Music and sugar make me

crazy for everything but

the sugar always wears off.

Stop.

See the noise.

Shyness keeps us strangers.

Fortune makes us lovers.

You are the sun and

I'm your planet.

Love Tactics

Someone gave me this book.

It's called "Love Tactics -

How to Win the One You Want."

I don't dare throw it away.

What I Got

What I got is who I am.
I got a thousand CDs cos

the music is primary, essential.
I got a black cat named Boo

and a kitten named Louie.
We're a family.

I've got a guitar and a computer.
It keeps me plugged in,

while the phone
is mostly silent.

I go downtown.
I walk down the street in the November shade

of cool, tall buildings.
I'm a groovy little rat with someplace to be.

In my bag, I got style, I've got love,
Dr. Pepper and a banana,

some tapes for my head,
the Doors Greatest, Oasis Definitely Maybe,

Eric B. and Rakim Follow the Leader,
Radiohead, the first one,

the one with Creep.
and Pretty Hate Machine.

I sit down in the hallway
of the seventh floor and I wait for her.

The Sleepers 2.0

I wander all night in my dream,
My feet are wings, I softly swoop,
  Step and spin.
My eyes look behind theirs, the drawn shades
of sleepers.
I'm lost but unfazed… no destination… aimless
  Intuition is my guide.
I stop, jump, dance and dissolve into the fog.

How innocent are the sleepers, on king-sized
beds and sofas;
How quietly they breathe, children asleep in
the grass.

Sweaty drunkards in three-hour comas, the
dead in their graves,
  Broken bodies in ghetto hallways, crazy
people in padded cells,
Babies slip from their mamas' wombs, souls
ascend or descend,
  Checking in, checking out, this might be hell,
it might be heaven.
The night inhales them and they breathe it right
back.

The happy couples sleep like spoons in a
drawer,
  The kids and their dog sleep down the hall,
Certain of milk and sugar in the morning,
  And certain of their safety.
The men dream football and strippers,
  The ladies dream money and shoes.

The stalker sleeps in his car outside her
apartment.
She wonders what he's thinking, she's given
up on sleeping,
  She stares at the ceiling, watches shadows
from TV.
Her phone rings, she almost screams, it rings
again and
  Then stops… she holds her breath… and
waits.
Love is torture, it comes and goes, lives and
dies without reason.

I stand with my hands in my pockets,
  I watch the sky turn from bruised to black.
A cloud passes in front of the smirking moon.
  It keeps secrets from us but I don't mind…
I've never understood anything.

Teenage boys dream darkly in frustrated
movies,
The madman sleeps secretly, locked in,
shades drawn.

Poor people sleep on crowded mattresses,
The well-off sleep deeply in suburban palaces.
  I float near the ceiling. I see everything.
Little black babies, little white babies
Have the same dreams, whisper the same
prayers
  In their tiny, invincible hearts.

Everyone looks the same in the dark,
everyone's a little afraid…
What if we don't wake up tomorrow?
  Some worry, Well, what if we do?

In asylums and jails they sleep off whiskey and pills,
Dreamless and warm for a change... but
  The medicine always wears off.

I go from bedroom to barracks... from basements
To the penthouse, I watch the movie star shiver naked
  In her dreams of home...
I am the breeze in your curtains, I am the lightning,
I am the rain... the wind blows my spirit
  Across the puzzle of the sky.

The bus drivers, the lawyers, the dealers and the saints,
Doctors and thieves, poets and monsters,
  Lie softly and silent in the anonymous night...
The king himself has dreams while he sleeps...
A nightmare... of bombs and planes and exploding towers,
  He wonders if he is responsible...

And I soar above the mountains and the mountains sleep too,
I splash in the lake and it doesn't awaken...
  God sleeps bravely... puts his faith in us.
In the morning my heart escapes into space... the blue, black mystery,
The ceiling of sun and stars... and my soul...
  My soul hears cartoons in the kitchen.

How beautiful are the sleepers... dangerous and innocent,

Children and killers rise and greet the
American dawn.

Daybreak Summer

An explosion remains

on the horizon.

The misty city

lies sleeping.

It's always been this way.

Love shines down,

surrounds

my tiny groove.

The Best Poet

I'm the best poet.
I step up to the mic and
I've already lost.
I've been high all day.
I'm hungry and broke.
In my backseat, I
have an odd collection of
books and CDs,
tapes and t-shirts,
a dirty white tambourine.
The phone rings
every few days.
Yes, I'm the best poet.
My mother's still crying.
My father still hates me.
I owe everyone money and
I've nowhere to go, but
somehow
I convinced myself that
I'm much, much better than you.
The future holds me down.
It keeps me here,
paralyzed
in this everlasting moment,
not doing anything.
I don't need anyone but
this black cat on my lap.
I've got love and magic.
I step to the mic,
my eyes red with joy.
I'm dying
right
now.

Girlfriend

Back when my job was still drinking,
we went to Jeff Kaminsky's place one
afternoon,
a tiny, little shithole by the Menard's in
Richfield,
right in the shadow of the freeway,

We got exceptionally drunk,
remarkably drunk
like we do,
like I did.
Jeff soon passed out.
(No one can drink like Two Harbors kids.)

Tommy and I decided we should find Jeff's
stash of porn and
put a tape in the VCR.
Instead, hidden at the bottom of his closet,
under a rank pile of clothes,
we found a forlorn, deflated blow up doll.

We stole it, of course.
We brought it back to the dorm and blew her
up, but sadly,
it had a slow leak.
So she was slutty and vivacious for 10 or 15
minutes and then
pssssssssss.
Her perky, plastic breasts caved in and
flattened.

I felt bad for Jeff.
Not only had we stolen his girlfriend,
but she was broken and useless

(not unlike a regular person).
Apparently,
he had fucked her with such passion and vigor
that
she couldn't take it.

Imagine the look on his face,
trying to finish as she lay there under him.
Psssssssss.
Such a strange, desperate experience and
no one to share it with

Imagine the look on his face when
he couldn't find her and realized
she was gone.

Untitled

We light candles

at the foot of the bed.

This is the Divine Church of Sex

and I worship you here.

Supernova

This is what I do every Saturday morning.
I come here, sit down at this table,
wait for the muse,
her divine, little nudge.

My pen starts to move,
writing poems about you again.
Everything begins there and
everything ends there too.

I want to die and go to heaven
so I can see you again.
Sometimes that's the only thing
that keeps me going.
You are a supernova.

Work, sleep.
Work, sleep.
Work, sleep.

Last night I dreamed riots and secrets,
woke up tired,
got in my car and came here.

Meanwhile,
you are on the other side of the ocean.
You kiss your children.
You fuck your husband.
You haven't thought about me
in years.

Back in the Day

Back in the day, we survived

on comedy, coke and casual love.

2 A.M. at Ember's, we ordered pancakes and

cheesy hash browns.

We smoked incessantly and our waitress

was a saint.

All revved up, we arrived at the party,

our hearts dark and beautiful.

We found shiny, plastic women with

not so plastic accessories.

You winked at me before leaving.

We were unkind at times,

me more so than you, and you

saved me always from the mystery of

my obsession.

You ensured that I stayed alive during this

relentless experiment.

I dug you for that then and still.

You were my movie star.

The city was on fire and the city

was the source,

the inspiration and you were its master.

We stood on the bridge and watched the

bodies swirl under.

Bad Night

Like most beautiful things,

this was random and divine.

He stared up at the ceiling.

watching the shadows and swirling light.

"What is that all about?" she asked.

"Someone's getting arrested, I think.

Someone's having a bad night."

"Not me, she murmured. "Not me."

Like a strobe on a mirror ball,

the lights from the police car lit up the room.

The universe took their picture,

over and over and over.

Something to Do

The boulevard is piled with jagged scoops

of Oreo ice cream.

A river flows down the edge of the street.

10-year-old boys race popsicle sticks.

My dad's old truck splashes past,

almost hits us.

My dad doesn't wave.

There's work to be done.

There's always something to do,

even while the world is dying.

David

What was David thinking,

the night before,

or walking there,

the second during,

the eternity after?

Did he have second thoughts

in mid-air?

Was there regret

or only relief?

The moment when you decide:

This is what I'm going to do.

This is how I'll fix it.

That exact moment is

an emotion that

doesn't have a name.

You will never know it exists

until you feel it.

David decided.

He's gone and now

he's everywhere.

Brooke and Jennifer, Tracy and Tonya

In 1990,
4 gorgeous girls
dominated hipster culture in Duluth.
They were the alternative girls,
the anti-cheerleaders,
all charisma and
style.
The sidewalks, streets and hallways
were their runways and
stages:
From the art department at UMD
to Canal Park,
from Chi Chi's to the Emerson School,
from the Hacienda to the Fetus,
from the mall to downtown,
the east side, the west end,
the NorShor to Sir Benedict's,
RT Quinlan's to the Global Village,
Park Point to the Anchor Bar.
Everyone knew them or of them and
most of us worshipped them.
They exuded art and music.
They didn't need us.
They were models,
arbiters of fashion and
taste.
They smoked a little weed,
had some drinks from time to time,
had boyfriends
or not.
It didn't really matter.
They listened to the Pixies and
Smashing Pumpkins and
Lou Reed,

back when the rest of us were listening to
Bon fucking Jovi.
These girls clearly mattered to me,
because 1000 years later,
I can't forget
Brooke and Jennifer, Tracy and Tonya.

Rumi

I figured if

I read her

the perfect Rumi poem

with melody,

cadence and

stars in my eyes,

that she would smile and

(silently)

leap into my arms.

We would fall in love,

forever after,

watch the sunrise glow

through the curtains.

So, I've been searching

through his poems,

making notes and rehearsing,

waiting

for the moment

to tell you.

The Basement Diary

My buddies live upstairs.
I envy them, hell yes.
They've jobs and futures,
girlfriends, checkbooks and big sacks of weed,
which they ignore somehow,
for days at a time.
Me, I sleep in the basement.
I've a stack of dirty magazines and
some stolen cigarettes.
I drink drink drink and
sometimes I drink with the boys,
but they can't keep up.
They seem to enjoy a mutual reality.
It's always late.
I'm suddenly sick and sleepy and
these guys have to work in the morning.
I write a shitty poem on a cardboard box.
I see spiders in my shoes.
I hear them laughing upstairs.
I just want to be pure.

My Hero

My hero sat across the table,

lit one of my cigarettes and

read aloud the sports section,

pausing to tell me about our super fresh

waitress and her mysterious past.

My hero introduced me to LL Cool J,

showed me where to park Uptown,

where the best Dairy Queen was.

He lent me his Chuck Taylors

during that endless, high-speed summer.

My hero and I buzzed around in his Jeep

shouting disco sing-a-longs

during a weekday quest

to meet dope, middle aged

executive assistants.

We did ecstasy on Portland Avenue and

grooved until dawn

with suburban girls named Amber and Blair.

My hero had an apartment in the clouds.

He had a planet for a playground.

Last January, my hero moved to Los Angeles

and now,

no one reads me the sports.

Sailing

I remember my fearless young self,
high on a bicycle, 14 years old, thinking,
"This is what it's all about."

My life, your life, everything and
when passion, faith and true love
disappear into the dark,

I think of you, me and slow dances.
I breathe the warm, sweet, spring wind and
I go sailing though space and time.

Soul to Soul

I see you sitting across the room and
I wanna take you home,
like a prize,
like a possession.
I wanna wrap you up.
You and me,
we're the same.
We've been to the bottom.
We paid a price.
We stared at the ceiling
wanting to die,
wanting to live,
doing neither.

We tortured ourselves
while we watched the stars
revolving around us.
You and me,
we're connected.
I'm attracted to you
magnetically and
magically.
I want to take care of you.
Listen.
Sleep.
Dream.
Feel your heartbeat.
Offer you a massage
in a shameless, obvious ploy
to put my hands on you,
to kiss your cream shoulders,
to taste the soft curve of your neck.

We understand each other a little bit and

that's enough for me.
But on the other hand,
I don't really know you at all.
You are an exquisite mystery.
I'd like to break you down.
Get inside you.
Bring out your animal.
Hear those happy screams,
then stare at the ceiling
together.

Deep Thought

Who do you think Archie should be with?

Betty or Veronica?

It's a tough call.

Both have their strong points.

Betty is pretty, pure and wholesome.

She is innocent.

She is springtime.

I bet she volunteers at the retirement home,

brings blankets, cookies and tea.

works long hours and accepts no pay.

At home,

she does the dishes after dinner,

helps her little brother with his homework,

keeps her bedroom tidy and clean.

Betty is an angel.

It's no wonder Archie digs her.

But I think he should choose Veronica,

cos she's rich, man, and

I bet she puts out.

Starry Night

I wonder what goes on

behind your eyes.

Have you seen the future

back there, out there, somewhere?

Have you ever skipped to the part

where you and I are tangled together,

whispering kisses and laughter,

deep inside each other

on an endless starry night?

So, tell me, stranger,

did you ever dare

skip to the part with

the happy ending?

C'mere.

Fast Forward

I've had the same dream

since I was 15,

standing on

a deserted softball field,

the autumn wind offering up

my heartbreak melody.

The only thing

that's changed is

now

I know

your name.

Duluth Summer

Wake up.
Make coffee.
Toast a bagel.
Put a CD on.
Hit play.
Smoke a bowl.
Stare out the window.
Watch the traffic.
Get dressed.
Put your stuff in your bag.
Grab your volleyball.
Go downstairs.
Get in your car.
Roll the windows down.
Put a tape in.
Drive to Parker's.
Head for Park Point.
Smoke a bowl.
Stop at Bayside Market.
Buy Gatorade and Combos.
Drive to the Point.
Park car.
Lay out towel.
Smoke a bowl.
Play volleyball.
Get tan.
Laugh.
Sweat.
Smile.
Shine.
Thank God.
Repeat.

Phantom

I am a phantom,
a spirit,
a ghost.
I am walking down the hallway and
no one can see me.
The most beautiful girl in the world
walks toward me,
closer and then
passes right through me.
I sit in the coffee shop,
invisible,
a spectator,
writing shitty poems
on the back pages
of other shitty poems.
The phone hasn't rung in 18 years.
I shout silence.
It's okay.
I'm your conscience.
I keep track and
when this is all over,
these poems will indict you.
You'll cry a little bit,
feel sorry for yourself.
Then we will tear the poems up,
throw confetti in the air and
then you
will be a phantom
too.

Two Songs

#1

When I listen to the Blue Nile,
I come to at the Park Inn International.
I'm at the hotel by the lake
having dangerous sex with
the super fly Ice Capades chick.
She's the choreographer.
She smells like patchouli.
She tastes like strawberries.
She fucks like a cat.
We smoke some weed.
We do it again.
Meanwhile, across town,
my amazing girlfriend waits tables,
looks at her watch,
wonders for a moment
what I'm doing.

#2

When I hear the Candy Rain,
I'm on the beach again.
The hot summer wind stings our backs.
me and this beautiful Russian girl,
kissing like we know each other
(movie star kisses).
I won't go to work today.
I couldn't possibly.
I watch her sleeping in my bed.
She smells like CK One.
She tastes like the sea.

We will be madly in love
for one hundred hours.
Then she'll get on a plane and
disappear,
like a sweet hallucination,
like a dream we both had.
I keep our picture in my car
to remind me how good it was,
the reality, the past, the potential.
Half a world away,
she lies awake,
stares out the window
at the full moon.
We remember everything.

Simone the Jewish Vampire

Simone the Jewish vampire
has a formula for drama.
It starts in her vacant eyes.

It grows in her inaccessibility.
She draws her curtains and listens
to tragic, tainted melodies.

Simone the Jewish vampire
has a number of books on witchcraft.
They are mostly nonsense but

they enhance this clever pose.
Her best friend comes over to conspire and
they invent a secret language.

Simone the Jewish vampire
takes her friend for coffee at midnight.
They stay there for hours, smoking cigarettes,

professing decadence, grooving on
their complex natures and their jet-black nails.
The waitress loathes them.

But Simone the Jewish vampire
drives a shitty, rusty Honda and
I saw her bussing tables at the Green Mill.

Springtime in Duluth

Sterile, sane danger in long, skinny hallways,
in my neat, little cell,
I keep a picture of my family and
I stare at the glowing, gray eyes
of a groovier me.
I want to be innocent again.
I want to be inspired.
I have a schedule here, a daily routine.
I tremble from here to there
clutching my blue, plastic coffee cup,
labeled like everything here.
I'm ready for anything.
I have a roommate who came all the way
from Illinois to save himself.
He used to be bank president, but
he couldn't keep it together.
I relate to that.
I've been there.
My blood pressure seems very important.
I'm 5'10".
I weigh 167 pounds.
A doctor will stop by tomorrow and vacantly
make note of these facts.
For 28 days I drink decaf coffee.
I smoke 1,000 cigarettes and
thank God for them.
I wear sweatpants, all day, every day.
I make my bed at dawn and I ache
for music or a TV.
There is someone standing by the elevators
and
I can hear everything.
His name is Don J. and he
left the day before yesterday.

He's all fucked up, can't even talk but
I know what he's saying.
I pull a pillow over my head, so afraid that
I pray to God or anyone who's listening,
Please tell me we can do this.
How do you feel?
someone asks again,
relentlessly.
I feel like Don J., I say,
crazy in that jungle
we can't stop exploring.

Romantic

You and me,
we are
romantic

animals.
We howl and we claw.
We purr and we roar.

We kiss sweetly too,
fingertips tracing
circles on skin.

We whisper made up words and soon
our bodies are
dancing together.

You and I are
a gun and a rose.
We are romantic little cavemen,

dirty, little bunnies,
happy, happy,
happy.

Untitled

On the bus today,

I felt the universe

enter through my left ear and

exit through my right.

I'm born every morning.

Summer

I plugged in a breeze and

listened to the cars whiz by.

I wish for a safer, saner hobby and I'm

thinking of ice cream sandwiches.

I told someone at work that I need a life and

she said that she

thought I had one.

No, I have a suntan. It's not the same thing.

And I keep this nameless passion still.

It keeps my heart beating and discerns

meaning and reminds me I'm okay

with immaculate timing.

Style, you see, it's style I seek and of course,

someone to kiss.

Super Fuzz

Me and this goofy guy from work
decided to start a band.
We decided to name it Super Fuzz,
which I thought was a solid name.
Naming the band is really important.
Otherwise, you could end up with
a good band with a stupid name,
like Foo Fighters or Goo Goo Dolls.
Alas, it turned out that my co-worker was
goofier than I could handle.

So I'm still looking to start a band.
The flyer will read:
Super Fuzz seeks like-minded power poppers*
to play guitar, bass, drums, keys and harmony,
fill stadiums or coffee shops
with songs about love, pain and other drugs.
Please have your own gear and
twisted little dreams.
Open mind required.
*Must know at least 3-5 chords.

I'll put this flyer up at Dunn Brothers,
Cheapo and Roadrunner.
Maybe post it on Craigslist, too.
Weeks or probably months later,
the phone will ring and
it will be that goofy fucker from work.
Damn.
I'll say, Okay, but I'm the lead singer.
Got it?

Saturday

At the crosswalk,

she appears to me.

In jet black shades, she's

a movie star, my angel.

She turns the corner.

I will never know her name.

My heart is dizzy.

In the coffee shop

the newlyweds kiss their baby.

Last night,

the rain washed the street.

Summer is singing.

The door lets in

a spectacular breeze.

Nirvana

Daniel called late Wednesday morning.

Billy is going downhill, he said, and

he's picking up speed.

It's a strange and beautiful day:

love and loss,

beauty and chaos,

a day like any other,

except that

Billy's checked into hospice and

started a morphine diet.

We share pictures of happy times.

We say kindest words.

Billy sleeps in the light.

There's no pain here.

When years dissolve into days,

we can't help but laugh.

We remember everything.

Billy's mom hears testimony of

his finest moments,

his wisdom,

his epic feats.

Outside, the sun pounds on the windows.

Billy breathes in love,

exhales peace.

The TV is on the Twins game,

volume down.

No one's watching.

We tell his stories,

like the time he was walking past

the open doors of the Uptown,

heard guitar, drums, thunder,

went inside to investigate,

saw Nirvana playing

to an empty room,

looked Kurt right in the eye.

I can hear drums right now.

I can hear Kurt singing.

Billy starts to hum.

Disappear

You understand now
why watching football
brings me more joy
than your company.

I'd rather spend the weekend
with a stack of Hustler magazines and
a handful of lotion than here,
locked in your screaming hotel.

You hate me now.
When you told me you loved me,
I knew it would pass.
I knew we would get here,

that you would hate me like this.
You understand now.
I'm full of poison and spit.
I'll end up alone.

I'm already here.
Think I'll start smoking again.
Leave the TV on.
I'll fade away.

Hate simplifies.
Love complicates.
Nothing matters.
We disappear.

This

I bought this shirt cos
I like the way it looks.
I look like I'm famous.

I put on this record cos
I like the way it sounds.
This melody fills me up.

I bought this book cos
I like what it says.
The words build a fire inside me.

I like this movie cos
I know these people.
They walk in and out of my story.

I like this girl cos
my eyes get drunk
when I look at her.

I like this weather cos
It blows my soul into the stars
like a kite without a string.

On Sunday

The kids arrived after lunch on Sunday.
There were usually two or three buses,
but it was mostly mini-vans and
Japanese cars.
Mom and Dad dropped off their young
Lutherans
for a week of Jesus and mischief.
I was their counselor.
I was there to help,
to teach them,
make their faith stronger.
However,
I was a train wreck.
I was a time bomb.
Usually when I met the kids
I was still sweating out the weekend,
hard, hazy chaos and blackouts.
The other counselors would tell me what I did
on Saturday night.
I would nod and say,
Yes, that sounds like me.
I wore a Miller Lite t-shirt and
I smoked cigarettes
whenever I could get away for 5 minutes.
I was a terrible counselor, but
man, I loved those kids.
They were wide open,
funny, fearless, full of life,
5-foot heroes with big, high voices.
I would be cool when I met them, but
later on, I would yell at someone for something.
Then they would be a little bit afraid of me.
In theory, I was there to teach them, but
in reality, they taught me.

God pumped them up
like birthday balloons and
they flew into the sky.
I am thankful for those lessons.
On Sunday afternoon, the parents
gave us their wise little children.
We became a family for 6 days,
holding hands,
sharing meals,
hitting baseballs,
swimming in our miniature sea.
At night we sang praises and
the fire sent up sparks
that turned into stars.
I can still see the world
through those 10-year-old eyes:
running, laughing,
shouting with joy
like puppies barking.
Thanks to them,
I'm still innocent somehow.
I've been forgiven.
I'm still enchanted by this life.
I'm still hypnotized by
the memory of
the orange, gold glow
of the summer sun
dissolving into
that silver lake.

Falling

Say, Please.

Please.

Say, Pretty please.

Pretty please.

Say, Honey, I love you so much.

You're the most beautiful girl in the world and

my life is meaningless without you.

Honey, I love you so much.

You're the most beautiful girl in the world and

my life is meaningless without you.

Okay, she smiled, okay, and

slipped her pink panties slowly

past her hips and then

dropped them off the side of the bed

carefully,

so she could find them

in the morning.

Hurricane

Cars break down.
Flowers die.
Lightning strikes.
Babies scream.

Another headache.
Jesus is exhausted.
Bones break.
Airplanes crash.

People kill people.
Dogs fight cats.
Cats hunt mice.
The stars implode.

"I don't feel well," he said.
"I don't feel well at all."
He closed his eyes.
He lay down to rest.

Cars break down.
Hearts stop ticking.
Thunder booms.
There's a hurricane in my head.

Highway 36

The sun sets in my rearview mirror.

The devil dances on the seat beside me.

I cross my heart. I hope to die.

I spit resin in the sink.

I smoke in the health club parking lot.

I wasted Wednesday afternoon

making love to the girls who

arrived in the mail that morning.

The dreamer lies dying in the alley.

I'm still here.

Broken

Here's the deal:

She'll never break my heart cos

that fucker's always broken.

Chuck Taylor

Chuck Taylor liked to smoke weed,

lots of it, all day, every day.

It was like breathing now,

a miniature fog bank that made his head

a little fuzzy, a little muddy,

a little better and

a little worse.

He knew deep down that

it was a trick, that

this Pauly Shore movie he was watching

was neither clever or funny,

that he should really be at work,

that his money could be better spent,

that he had no business driving.

Chuck Taylor was not to be deterred.

He kept 99 moods

in a baggie on his dresser.

He ignored the phone when it rang.

He smiled at the police officers

who drove slowly past.

He paid his rent and worked

hard enough to maintain

this sacred state of mind

indefinitely.

The beach was buzzing with color and sound.

Wearing 5-dollar mirrored sunglasses,

Chuck Taylor lay in the sun,

sipping a grape Gatorade,

watching a volleyball game.

He and Brady had next.

There was music in the air and

he sang along.

A year passed.

Chuck Taylor thanked God

for everything,

went home and

fell asleep

in a dreamless cloud.

Hard Work

Do you want to hear my secret plan?
We jump.
We leap because we're fearless.
I promise, we will land like feathers
on water.
We can make love until morning,
tentatively, sweetly,

then
we can do it like race cars
for half an hour,
loudly,
deeply.
We will make a fire.

Are you tired of feeling hollow,
like we're running on a treadmill?
We circle the same rooms
like zombie goldfish,
watching the clock
turn into a calendar.

Let's be the brave ones.
Let's be the crazy motherfuckers
who fall in love.
Happiness is hard work and
I am going to kiss you
until the sky shatters.

33

There are 33 plants in this corner.

We exchange puffs of imported air.

I watch the door open and close.

My coffee is magnificent,

bigger than my head,

as big as my heart.

Gooey, chocolate electricity and

I'm 12 years old now,

making up stories

with me as the hero

and you as you.

The Magic Poem

She said, "Wow!
That was the best poem I've ever heard.
You touched my heart and I
totally love you now.
Let's go in the bedroom and
make love for seven days."
I said, "Sure!"
Thank God for the magic poem.
And yeah, I know it was just a dream, but
is that really any different than
a memory?

Miss Julie Right

I have plans for us, Julie.

Let's start a fire in the corner.

Let's make chocolate chip cookies.

Let's write sultry, sweet poems for each other

with lipstick on our walls.

Let's light a candle and wait for Jesus.

Let's go on long, windy walks

by an ancient sea.

Let's get lost on a map,

walk straight into the sun on a blinding beach.

I'll tell you stories until you're sleeping.

I'll wash our clothes.

I'll make our bed.

I'll kiss you, kiss you, kiss you.

We will be born again

on a neon Ferris wheel.

I'll make cinnamon toast for breakfast.

I'll write 100 songs about you.

You and I would be heroes and angels,

all this because

you are my reward,

my soft paradise.

12

One time,
when Todd was 12,
he discovered a stack
of Playboy magazines
in the basement at the house
where he was babysitting.
He was transfixed.
This was the 70s, so
the models had pubic hair and
their boobs were real.
These images filled his mind
quickly and completely,
like a balloon filling with helium.
He didn't stand a chance.
At that precise moment,
Todd became
an idiot.

Out of Breath

Out of breath, dizzy, crazy,
all the feelings that she gave me.

Sad and angry, lost and lonely,
how I felt when she first told me.

Out of breath, dying slowly,
acting like she doesn't know me.

She destroyed me, killed the dream,
out of breath, I try to scream.

If there was a perfect moment,
one that I could frame and own it,

a single, sacred memory
would be enough to set me free.

If she would call me one more time
with some excuse, some worn out line,

I would be quick to forgive her,
order flowers to deliver,

sing the songs that make her laugh,
buy a cookie, give her half.

If she would park outside my door,
I could find a little more

love like white wine, rain and sunshine,
paintings, photos, valentines.

Out of breath, dizzy, crazy,
all the feelings that she gave me.

Lottery Ticket

Remember?

Back in the day,

crossing Tower Avenue

between the Cove and

the Casablanca?

You would ask a girl to dance.

It was terrifying.

It was so loud that

you had to scream into her ear:

DO YOU WANNA DANCE?

After, if you were lucky,

you got her number.

She would say,

Do you have a pen?

You would ask the bartender

or the waitress to borrow theirs.

She would write her name and number

on a cocktail napkin.

You'd thank her,

tell her you'd give her a call.

She would smile and

disappear back onto the dance floor.

You would look at this number like

it was a launch code,

valuable and dangerous.

You would try to memorize it quickly,

in case the napkin was lost or torn.

It was like a lottery ticket

in your pocket.

When you got home,

you would set it carefully

on the dresser and

promise yourself

not to call too soon.

Heather, you would say to yourself,

dreamy and sleepy,

as you faded slowly into slumber.

Her name is Heather.

In the morning,

the first thing you would do is

check the dresser,

make sure it was real.

Watching TV

God watches us on cable TV.
He's like, "WTF?"
Sometimes He watches football, but
He steadfastly refuses to cheer
for Notre Dame,
or impact the outcome in any manner.
He watches The Real Housewives
of Beverly Hills and
Atlanta and
dislikes all of them equally.
He loves The Price is Right.
He's embarrassed that He watches The
Bachelor,
just like the rest of us.
God channel surfs.
He watches Aleppo on CNN and
He wonders about free will.
He turns to ESPN.
He loves SportsCenter,
watches as LeBron and Zion W. go off.
He prefers pop culture over high art.
He hates bro country.
He feels bad about Prince.
He hopes Oasis get back together, but
so far has been unwilling to intervene.
God watches Animal Planet, HGTV and
movies on HBO.
He likes SNL, Jim Gaffigan,
Dave Chappelle and Chris Rock.
He hates all the Christmas specials,
except the Charlie Brown one
(kinda).
God yawns,
turns His TV off

with His universal remote,
goes into the kitchen
to make a snack.

All That Matters

People jump off ledges

high above the street.

Dogs get crushed by cars.

People kill people

with guns,

with knives,

with their bare, raw hands.

Trains come off their rails and spill destruction

onto the morning commute.

Mom is screaming at her children.

Dad is in prison for you know what.

Your pilot is badly hung over.

You can be replaced at work.

Your poetry is god awful.

So is the music you listen to

and the movies you watch.

Your socks don't match.

You have crumbs on your shirt.

You didn't wash your hands.

Your teeth hurt.

You're rank.

A beautiful bird crashes hard into the window.

The model can't keep food down.

She's coughing up blood.

The president is an asshole.

We're all going to die.

The doctor killed his patient

because he checked his email

during open heart surgery.

Mom and Dad are divorced now.

The children hate them.

The house is on fire.

He drinks too much.

She can't keep her legs closed.

Rich, white men pass laws

to make themselves richer.

Someone shoots one of them in the face.

The sky glows danger.

The best player on your favorite team

just shredded his knee.

You slip and fall down the basement stairs.

Your arm snaps like pencil.

Your 3-year-old drowns

in the neighbors' pool.

All of this is happening,

all day,

every day.

This is the world we live in.

I don't care about

any of it.

All that matters to me

is this tiny, gray kitten

peeking

out

from the patio door.

Dirty Job

It's a strange position.
Being a poet means
you have to pay attention.
You have to drink a lot and
do a certain amount of drugs
but then you have to quit.
You have to forgive everybody.
You have to stop spitting at
yourself in the mirror.
You have to read books.
You can never give up.
Watch the families leaving church.
Their lives are pure cinema.
Watch this wrinkled old man
shut the door to the bathroom stall.
He has a small, brown, paper bag and
he is smiling
for now.
Watch the traffic go by.
They are sheep that learned to drive.
It's up to you to save them.
Feel it.
Take it.
Smother little bombs in your chest and
write them down later
in a spiral notebook.
You finally admit that you miss your dad.
You should have done things
differently.
You want to call your mom.
The wind smells like a carnival.
The music plays between your ears
at all times,
It doesn't stop.

It's the soundtrack to your life.
The most beautiful girl in the world
pours you a cup of coffee.
You're so sad you're happy.
You cry until you feel good.
You drive down the street you grew up on and
you can feel the sun in your stomach.
You're on a mission.
You're Charles Bukowski's bastard child.
You're a warrior from the ancient plains.
Go ahead.
Jump off this building.
You will fly.
You can't kill a poet.

"We all want something beautiful. Man, I wish I was beautiful."

- Counting Crows, Mr. Jones